something like forgiveness

something like forgiveness

poems by
rebecca schumejda
art work by
hosho mccreesh

Stubborn Mule Press
Devil's Elbow, MO
stubbornmulepress.com

All poems copyright © Rebecca Schumejda 2019
All artwork copyright © Hosho McCreesh 2019

First Edition 11 7 5 3 2 1
ISBN: 978-1-950380-37-4
LCCN: 2019942213
Design, edits and layout: Jeanette Powers
stubbornmulepress@gmail.com @stubbornmulepress
All Artworks: Hosho McCreesh
Bio Photo, RS: Kaya Lanier
Bio Photo, HM: Freddie De La Cruz

Are you really reading this? Congratulations, we love you. No one but the author can really claim rights to their work, no matter what law says what. And we can't really do anything about theft, whatever that means, so here is our pact: Be cool, be kind, don't steal, email the author if you like or want to riff off their work. Also, let us at Stubborn Mule know if you want to write a review, we'll share it and your review publication, too. Go ahead and use passages for reviews, accolades, or epigraphs, give credit where credit is due. Let's stay radical, share with us our honor among anarchists.

For Ted Jonathan

I would like to thank Daniel Crocker, John Dorsey, Lynne Savitt and David Kaczynski for encouraging me to write when it hurt the most.

The boy you were   cradles a rifle
waits patiently   in a tree stand
there are birds   the boy wishes
he could identify   like our father did
the sun comes up   coffee in thermos
lukewarm   you hear leaves
crunching
you hold the rifle
    like a hammer
        like disappointment
            like you didn't mean to

take aim

shame hangs
like a deer carcass   limp and lifeless
    like her laughter
        like who I was before
           like who I am becoming

I move and move and keep on moving

we fix one house
    then move onto
        another broken down one

this current house we are working on
reminds me of   how life goes on
after death   the ongoing
construction   reminder of
what has been lost   the possibility of
what will be   the long process
involved

forgiving
    you

    is like using a feather
        as a hammer
            as a rifle

                        a
                        f
                        e
                        a
                        t
                        h
                        e
                        r

believing you can
fix
anything
        reconstruct a home
                a relationship
                        your words
to fit in with who you are now
                who you will be
                      who you were
and never were

how the p, g, and y hang low
        in apology
                like upside-down antlers

there are seconds
in each minute that I want to
disappear behind the tree line

        come back innocent

but I come back
either too light   or too heavy

like conversations we have
on a recorded line
    or letters read by guards
        who monsterize you

are they listening   now
are they
        all those men behind a forest
are they
        of bars, forgotten
listening
are they

I start another letter to you:
dear 16B0527
I think forgiveness is both feather and hammer and I
can't stop thinking about what they say you did what
you say you did what was done and why

as much as I know I don't know I know I don't

I am driving home
I am always   driving home,
but I never get there

instead I fall asleep

the sound of wings
    startled by a shot fired
        a deer grazed by a bullet

    runnnnnning now running
clumsily more legs than body more body than legs
I run toward the tree line I run and run and run

until I realize it's the cat
he must have knocked something over

differing degrees of "goony eyes," and further appall society with their resultant behavior and crimes.

he wants to be scratched behind the ears
                        to go outside
                        before sunrise
he hears birds chirping

after I descend the stairs
turn the corner
I step into a tray of paint
                        the paint
last night, my husband
didn't come to bed
                        reminds me of
he was up late painting
the ceiling   all the evidence
                       that makes no sense

the mess left behind

the cat circles me
meowing   like you
meowing
he wants nothing more
than to be outside

I take off my socks
try to limit the damage

when he rubs against me
        I feel so alone

is touch how you figure out
        who is there
                and who is not

                because sight
                        and sound
                                deceive you

I am here

but you can't touch me
so am I really here

    if you call

                                      who
                                      are
                                      you
                                      talki
                                      ng
                                      to

        who is listening

there is still so much   construction
left to do   how will we
my heart   get it done
        ladders and nail guns
                sadness and guilt
                        buckets of paint
                              anger
                      cans of screws
                            regret

                    drills
              disbelief
        hammers
exposed wires

forgiveness is a total gut

when you expected
a simple remodel

over four years later
and still piecing it together

and the to-do list is growing
    time is the wound
    don't bullshit me
    about healing

sometimes it is better not to know
what is hiding
behind the walls
        behind that familiar face
    a labyrinth of rat holes
        those hands you trusted
    animal droppings
    bones
    nests
    mold
    fur
        some kind of monster

there is never enough insulation
to protect us
from this crazy world

inside the mind
a labyrinth of conspiracy theories

        shadows
        an arsenal of voices
        a school of killies
        swimming in murky water
        on a sunny day

cup your hands and try to catch
the light coming in
through your barred window

fins like wings flapping   close your eyes
can you hear   waves crashing

against concrete walls   all the pills
are fish left on the shore   they give you to
quiet the space between   your demons
trembling fingers   you close your eyes
but your eyelids   are movie screens
    projecting nonstop memories

the cat crouching behind some   bushes
my children are still sleeping
my oldest is afraid of falling   asleep now—
I read and respond to emails   what can happen
google ghost symptoms   when you close
your doors   your eyes
self-diagnose a disease   I am afraid
to wake her   afraid
that where she is   is safer
than here, now

instead
keep busy, keep busy
do a load of laundry
pile tools into one pile
instead of fifty
and organize a sock drawer

    don't make time
    for thoughts
        forget
            this is not
            procrastinati
            on

            this is
            survival

use the edge of a razor
to peel dried paint off tiles

I should finish the letter I started   I am
scared of you   morphing
of how you interpret   my words
into something sinister   the empty
inside me that I filled with   forgiveness
leaked the runny yolk of   a sun
that comes up   from behind
the trees   scared boys
the dark shadows of men
                stand up, stand up
lined up for morning count
                they're coming

all those bad decisions
waiting to be accounted for
by number   the castles
not by name   you make
with commissary playing cards   I am sorry

I can't protect you   how the guards
I never protected you   intentionally
I didn't know   knock
this could happen to us   over castles

52 pickup   twice a day   for twenty
      something   years

before you lost your freedom
did you believe what dad said:
everything can be taken from you
except your mind

these words were not his
but he said them so often
they became his

I forgive you	a feather
I forgive you	a hammer
I forgive you	a black cat
I forgive you	wet paint
I forgive you	her laugh

the demons tossing your thoughts
like guards tossing cells

what is it that they are looking for anyway

a house	a castle
a castle	in a cell
a cell	you call
home	I don't
a tree stand	answer
leaves crunching	under the
weight of	loss

the more you do it
      like doing bird
the easier it gets
      like doing dry wall

    or painting rooms
    or loving
the unlovable   the unforgivable

or not saying sorry
for something
you don't remember doing

something I didn't do
but am being punished for

you weren't in your right mind

were you in your right mind

what rights
does a mind have

I should just go on

there is nothing I can do
to change what happened

if one more person asks

have you forgiven yourself

that cat in you
that brought home a feather
          eggs left unattended in nest

all those cards scattered across
the concrete floor
are boats
drifting in the bay

take advantage of a falling tide
wade into water
with a net
all those killies
you pull ashore
flopping in the sand

bait

to be hooked through the eye
cast into water
past those steel bars

there is a man next to you
who tells you he'll protect you
he says it won't cost you too much

oh wait
there is a feather
at the door
it is knocking
it wants to come in

there you are
back in the woods
mistaking sharks
for sparrows

there were trees

a lake

a toy fire engine

the one we don't talk about

the one with the ladder that extended

the one you were playing with

when someone who didn't

want to live any longer

locked herself in her room

and swallowed

a handful

of tiny

white

pills

mommy!

my daughter screams

and I run from room

                                        to room

to room

looking for the fire

        the flood

                the tornado

                      the broken glass

                          the blood

but when I find her
she is sitting on the couch
eating a banana

the peel on the floor
the TV on
the teenage mutant turtles
battling alien invaders
in the sewer system
I sit down next to her
put my arms around her

my life is like this
so chaotically mundane

if only the half-chewed banana
she force-feeds me
were some kind of communion wafer
something resembling forgiveness

(I know I should not say this, but
it would have been easier

                      did you hear that

on everyone
if you had just
killed yourself that night)

and I shouldn't feel guilty, right
      I am tired of picking up
            these pieces of beach glass
                her laugh
                      the smoothed edges

        left on the shore

        do you see that laugh

        do you reach out to touch that laugh

if I don't use question marks
        then I am not really
        looking for answers

am I

second-hand guilt   and I miss her too
is the little girl   but don't feel like
afraid of antlers   I have the right to
hanging on the wall   miss her

a little girl
who thought that
evil resided in another house
on the other side of town   if it were
                                   one of my
                                   daughters

but I should be grateful, right
my words can still come and go
as they please
like cockroaches skittering
through your cell

you told me you caught one once
a giant cockroach
with your bare hands
you named him Maxwell
the name of my childhood pet
a Portuguese Water Dog

who kept jumping over the fence
to swim across the bay
to Shelter Island

you kept it, the cockroach
                            you are something like dead
trapped for days
                            but we can't bury you
then convinced it was dead
                            instead we answer
you lifted the plastic cup
                            collect calls from you
and it scurried away

and you couldn't chase after it
you watched it leave
like your freedom

like everyone you loved
you had to let it go   like a guard
the way I have to   after a cell toss
let you go

the way you have become
a shadow on a wall

the way I cry
                the way the seagulls come
until
                to take the killies left behind
I shake
                like fish flopping on sand
every cell in my body
                I want to tell them
the sound of a baton
                you are loved

dragged over steel bars

in the middle of the night
                they need to know

                someone loves you

the eggs, in the nest,
that never hatched

the way you cry
for yourself

because who else
do we cry for
but ourselves

for our own losses
well that's what
our paternal grandmother said
when our maternal grandfather died
I was only eight
she told me to stop
crying for myself
he's dead   death was a distant planet
there is no use
crying for the dead   I knew nothing about gravity

                          that keeps us from colliding

go outside and play
                     you count

she said
                     and I'll hide
you are alive

go
outside

go

outside

and

play

I thought she was mean
but now I know
she was preparing me
for what the tides of life
would leave on my shore

even though

I can't remember
what I ate yesterday for dinner
I remember her words

why do we remember
what we remember
forget
what we
forget

after your pet escaped   the man asked again
you held a pillow   are you ready for that
over your face   protection
so the other men
on your block
wouldn't hear you cry

and they do the same

cover their fears
with a state issued pillow
that smells like wet hay
and vomit

unless they are cactuses

there are a lot of cactuses
where you are

don't let those men   there is nothing I can do
rub against you   to protect you

you swear you will capture
another cockroach
but you haven't yet

    they taunt you
    by darting in
    and out
    like sunlight
               like voices
                              intangible

this isn't about what you did

it's about what I didn't

regret

that boy who lived down the hill
                      the woods that have been
when we were kids
                cleared since

the boy who took you into the woods
                    now a new development

                    of cookie-cutter houses
a cardinal on a branch
is a smile on a restless face

the snapping of twigs

the lie you accepted
you let this happened
it is your fault

secrets kept
for decades

the way
when you look up

through leaves
on a sunny day
it's as if you're peering
through a kaleidoscope

oh the way the world looks
through kid eyes
a marble rolling across
a dusty floor
under a couch

when you are on your
knees asking for
forgiveness

when it wasn't your fault

if you walk into the woods
you have to find your way out

leave a trail
mark your path

tell me there wasn't anything
I could do
that it wasn't my fault
because I am having a hard time
trying to live with this guilt

the cat waiting to pounce
is the heart of a man
doing his time

and the family waiting
for him
are the veins

is contraband hidden
that boy's fingers
under your tongue
prying your mouth open

the truth you kept

like a hook in your lip

running your fingers across

her laugh

forgiveness

is the house we are trying to
piece back together
before we move on

is the need to feel safe again
after something like this happens

is trying to forget the fact that
your mind and all the pills
everything can be taken from you
                                      dusty marbles

except your mind
                                      pushed back

and even that is arguable now
                                      with the tips of

on your knees
                                      transgressions

for what was taken from you

stop crying for the dead
       go outside
              go outside

and run your fingers
along the bark of a tree
tell me what you feel

                remember this is yours

all those cactuses in the yard

waiting for you to
brush up against them

you live in a place where wind
rain, snow, and sunshine cannot reach you

which one do you miss most

remember sledding down the hill
by our childhood home
through the woods

those same woods

how once we almost collided
with a tree, but dad shifted the sled

so he would take the brunt of the impact

what is love anyway
but taking the impact
for someone else

sometimes it's like watching
                           your heart pressed against
wind, rain, snow and sunshine from your cell
                         commissary playing cards

I forgive you
                  a castle and
I forgive you
                  a cockroach
I forgive you
                  all those wet pillows

it's still not working

when I tell my therapist
                       and I wish I hadn't
it would be easier if you had
                            said that
killed yourself that night
she writes a note
on a yellow legal pad

I don't remember ever being mad at you
for anything

until now

even after you did what you did
I wasn't mad

not at first   not for the first year
     or the second   or the third

because I didn't believe
you did it

the way the boy   how handcuffs must
grabbed your wrists   remind you of him
and pushed your hands   down
how could you have known

how could you have
known

that is what he wanted to show you

what makes people
snap

like twigs
beneath heavy steps

running through the woods
that day

no one was there
to help you

the birds nesting in trees
                          are you an accomplice
just watched
                          if you turn your head
or turned their heads
like how

the men in the cages
around you
                          it won't cost much
do now
when they don't want to see
what is happening to
one of the other inmates
what could happen to them

to you

I admit the cat was stalking something earlier
                          the guards heard him screaming
near the wild flowers
                          you told me
and I did nothing
                          they took their time getting to him
just went on

preparing dinner:

roasted turmeric chicken

                                        processed soy

meat like stuff

sautéed brussel sprouts

                                        brownish corn

baked potatoes

                                        something

                                        mushy and
                                        off-white

everything I enjoy
reminds me of everything

you're not allowed to have

like the smell of garlic and freedom

warmth on a chilly day

the ability to open a door
and pass through
without shackles
and guards
and guns
pointed at me

that same boy
much older than you
a little younger than me
french kissed me   *what are you doing*
in the backseat of the bus   *back there*
his tongue twisted
past my lips like a power drill

   I am in love with you he said

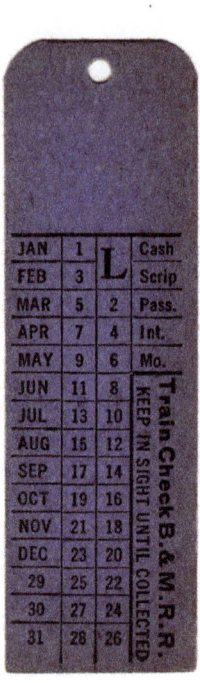
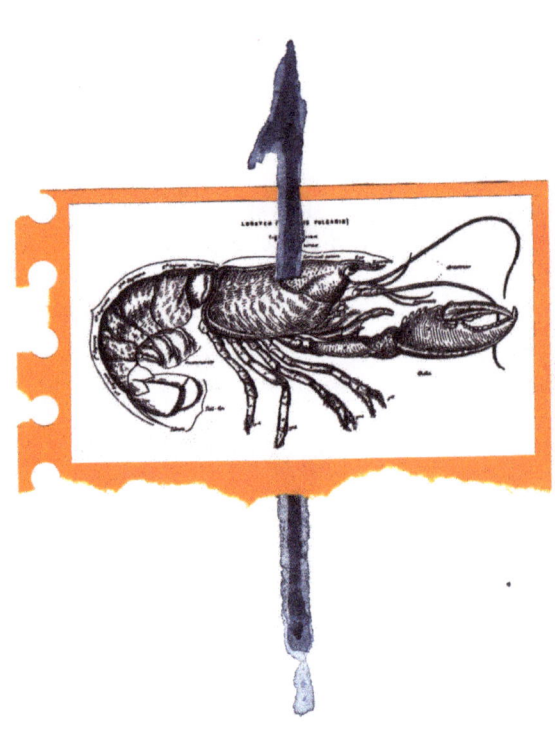

and I pulled the duct tape off
the hole in the seat
discover a stash of chewed gum

then let him kiss me
again

out of nowhere
my daughter asks me if
her eyebrows are growing together

like her father's
and I laugh so hard

I forget about
the cat

and you
about the feather
and antlers
and beach glass
and her laughter

and I say *no, but your hips*
are getting as big as his

and she laughs so hard
it's contagious
my youngest starts up
and we can't stop

snorting and all

this is healing
and it feels so good

this is something resembling
forgiveness

and I can't get enough of it
because I forget about that boy
                    those trees
how he asked me to be
                    in winter
his girlfriend and for a week
                    a closet full of
how I allowed him to follow me
                    skeletons
to my classes
let him hold my books
with those same hands
that wrapped around
your wrists
like shackles and pulled

your hands down

down
       down
              down

like oak leaves
      dropping from branches
fingers with nothing to grab onto
but air

my daughters
      the crunch dried leaves make
still laughing
      when you step on them
I think I hear myself
      still laughing too
      if only laughter
      were a life sentence

but then my youngest asks
if she can have an apple

before dinner and I hesitate
thinking about how
you're finally allowed real fruit
but when the guards inspect   and when we were kids
incoming packages   we'd take apples
they toss the apples and oranges
                               from the trees
mom brings you   before they were ripe
into the bottom of a canvas bag
                               we couldn't wait
before throwing aluminum cans on top

spite

is the opposite of forgiveness

this is the hand
        this is the feather
that pushed the weaker hand down
        on the wing
in the woods
        in the sky
while the birds watch
        strong as a hammer
or turn their heads
        this is me trying
but do not help
        to fly as far away as I can

most days my heart is a bruised red apple

I rinse a Red Delicious in the sink
dry it off on my shirt
hand it to my youngest

she bites through
tough skin

with baby teeth

she does not know you

you only held her once

against your
county issued orange jumpsuit
imagining she were
your own sons

the sons you will

probably never

see again

she is tired of the apple	there is so much left
she puts it down	so much wasted
and walks away

I can't imagine life
without my daughters
or how you must feel
knowing
you will never hand
your sons
an apple
watch them bite into
the world
take all of it in

you will not know
those simple pleasures

you throw a rotten apple	what a waste
at the concrete wall
and it explodes

that day

the only day

you will ever
hold my daughter
you handed her back
reluctantly
when the guard
started to stare

when she was back
in my arms
you reached out
and curled your fingers
around her tiny foot
as if it were a steel bar

all I want is for my daughters
to be able to hold on to
      the things they make
wind, rain, snow and sunshine
      that table you built in the shop
the way you held on to
      and the guard's family
her tiny foot
      who will set their dinner plates down
until we had to say goodbye
      on the hours you spent
I just want them
      making something that will never
to be able to
      be yours
cut through the skin
      like your sons
of this crazy world

with their teeth

and not have to depend on
knives
forks
me
spoons

I think about how you
              how almost anything can
aren't allowed silverware
              be turned into a weapon

for the next three decades
by desperate men

I wish I could twist
forgiveness
around the prongs of
a fork

and lift it
to my lips

open my heart
              that cell door
let it in
              that locks behind me
chew it up
              when I leave
and swallow
              but I never really leave

if I let the words
f
 a
  l
   l

from my mouth

like fish from the sky

trying to swim through air

I forgive you

forgive you

you

me, barbed wire
so much of who
        freedom and
we are
        the lack of
involves who
we aren't

when my daughter
        we grew up
knocks over
        under the same roof
her cup
and apple juice spills

a small stream
that waterfalls

onto the floor
                      what if you were just
I can feel dad's anger inside me
                angry not insane
a prisoner

trying to escape
through parted lips
the two cold steel bars

you grab onto
to hold yourself
steady

this is home now
now this is home
home is this now
is this home now

fuck I say

then grab a towel in lieu of
grabbing my youngest
and hugging her
as tight as I wish
our parents would have hugged us

when we needed it

most

I should have said

                        get help, go see someone

it's just apple juice

                        it's okay not to be okay

I love you

                        I love you

                                                  I
                                                  love
                                                        I
                                                                 love
                                                                       you

and
I   *forgive*   *myself*   *in*
you   *you*   *in*   *myself*

my daughter and apple juice
      you and the geese

and all the regrets I have
      migrating

spilling over my subconscious
      away from the cold

fuck, my youngest says
      how we learn things
a few minutes later
      how we repeat what we learn

and I remember how
      but regardless we were loved
much I just wanted
      and this makes no sense
to be hugged

tomorrow I vow to hug my daughters
at least three times
      to hug myself once

but when we wake up late
rush to dress
      I forget
brush hair
and teeth
pack lunches
shoes
   shoes
      shoes
where is the other
shoe
get one to daycare
the other on the bus
and by the time

I am driving away
I realize
I didn't even
say goodbye
and definitely
did not say

                        that small boy you were

I love you

                        the inmate you are now

forgive me

forgive me for letting them go
without telling them I love them

forgive me

I want for my children
what I didn't have
but I had so much
and that is why
I don't understand
how you could
do something
as disturbing
as you did

how

                                          how

could you

I will never know if that boy
took you into the woods

before
or after
I told him
I just wanted
to be friends

there is so much
you have buried
so much you don't remember

or say you can't remember

the space between trees
reminds me of loss
of your fingers wrapped
around branches
around steel bars
around that place
where the boy
pushed your hands
around my baby's toes
and if you hadn't held onto it
all those years
how would our lives
be different now

      would I check the locks
as if evil
      on the doors
is something outside of us
      over and over again
      each night
even though
what is inside
is what you should
fear the most

before going out to cut the lawn

for the last time this season
I put chili on the stove to simmer
my daughters are building a city
with Legos in their bedroom

they leave the windows open
yell to me as I drive
in figure eights around the muddy
backyard, hoping not to get stuck

life continues
without you

I don't see any birds out

not one

where are all the birds
when you need them most

all those feathers traveling
                      where were they that day
toward warmth
                      and why didn't they

                      swoop down
mommy!!!
                      and peck at his hands

did you do your homework I shout

and the window closes

then the tires get stuck
in the mud
and I have to get off
and push

push it out of the mud

like trying to push grudges
out of my mind

the same grudges
that migrated through
our dad's veins
like geese in fall

the V
and the honking
and the *don't forget*

look up
and remember
our childhood

when you look into
the autumn sky
through your barred window
do you see
cement clouds
or birds
traveling in the same direction
you are
away from home
or maybe back home

the only place you really live
is inside your own skin

is inside that moment
just before the rain
that steely gray before
tears
begin falling

that battleship gray

that shark gray

the skin of sky
the scales of a fish

can you hear
the drops hit
the window
over the roar of caged men

or her laughter
do you hear that laughter

which one breaks your heart more

before I left her office, my therapist says
it is alright to be angry,
we'll talk about it
in our upcoming sessions,
you did a good job today

I cry all the way home
my tears are the V geese make in the sky
speed up for a yellow light
then slam on my brakes
I could have made it

maybe I was the one
who let the cat out
that day he caught the cardinal

and I know that eventually
I will have to forgive
myself

and

you

not because
I accept what you did
but because
I can't accept
what not forgiving is doing to me

I thought forgiving you once
would be enough
but what no one tells you
is that forgiveness is a practice
that must be repeated
each day

sort of like prayer

for those who believe

I am sorry for giving you
          how we'd eat the cookie dough
forgiveness
          when mom turned her back
then snatching it back
          because even then we weren't afraid
like a child
          of death by raw egg
realizing that the cookie
they are about to give away
is the last one, so they pull back fast
put it in their mouth, swallow

recanted forgiveness on the tongue
tastes like baker's chocolate

          knowing you have someone

just one person

a red feather in a dry throat

in this world

let go! let go! let go!

you were my one person
it's orange beak against
black fur
trying to peck free
his hands
your hands
her hands

black feathers
and sometimes I wonder
wrestling
if you ever felt the same
with red fur

no

nO

NOOOOO!

forgiveness looks something like a construction site and sounds a little like

the woods at night   all those limbs falling

against their windowless souls

reminds me of what you and the other inmates
must look like lined up for evening count

```
            the light reflecting off
                        the metal toilet
                                    looks like a school of killies
                                                swimming in circles
                                                            arou
                                                            nd your
                                                            dingy cell

            you shout at your bunkie
                            you read somewhere that they
            for stomping on cockroaches
                            survived the ice age
            but you don't tell him why
                            those nasty creatures
            you just grit your teeth
                            that no one welcomes
            and wait for the opportunity
                            into their homes
            to catch one again

            you wait for me to visit
                            do you still see that Russian spy
            but I never come
                            the one who follows you

            I don't want to see you

            not the way you are now
                            the way you tremble
            I want to see you
                            from all of the anti-psychotics
            how you were
                            the way you look off into

                            the nothing

                            your life has become
```

I ask my therapist if
this is normal
to want to forget about
someone you love(d)
she says I should
visualize a visit

so I imagine you
a rare bird
flying in a straight line
through the visiting room
to where I am not sitting

you talk first

but I am not there to listen
                        maybe I am there
                        the nest that held the eggs
                        that never hatched
your red wings fold
like two hands in prayer
and I cup them in mine

you say sorry

        sorry sorry sorry sorrrrry
you understand that

you hurt us too

you say don't come back

then I get you a hamburger
from the vending machine
heat it up in the microwave
and bring it back to

where you were never sitting

you bite in
and it is frozen in the middle
but you don't care
this is the best meal
you've had in months

then you say *this was all a dream
wake up, wake up
you're going to miss your bus*

and I run and catch the bus
and that boy is in the backseat
but it is not really a backseat
it is the branch of a tree
and he holds out his hand
he says climb up
and I will bring you
to your brother
but I am afraid of heights
so I just stand there
watching fish drop
one by one
until there is a large pile
that I fall into

what do you see my therapist asks

and I see tangled knots
of barbed wire
a gun tower
gates
locks
steel

                                        and I see a little boy in line
                                        with a woman

                        she holds his hand
                        she asks him if he is excited
                        about seeing his father

and I see guards
who look through the little boy
as if he is a ghost
tugging the mother's arm
but the line keeps moving
I want to go home
                        almost every inmate says
                        they're innocent

and he is walking through the metal detector
and the alarm goes off
                        and the ghost and his mother
                        are taken aside

then our time is up
and my therapist is looking
at her calendar
telling me what dates
she has open

and even though time
is up, I tell her how
our father could not forgive
our sick uncle for not
making it to my wedding

how could he ever forgive you

for what you did

how

back at home
or a place that resembles it

I close the blinds, so my daughters
won't see the cardinal belly up
wings bent and broken
our cat licking himself clean
with his baptismal tongue

does forgiveness have a place in agnosticism

here's the thing about my wedding
        besides the fact that you helped
my husband and I pay for ten dance classes
        my husband write his vows
but only attended three
during our first dance
we held onto one another
and swayed
back and forth

we're still doing that
holding on

s
  w
    a
      y
        i
          n
            g

when my husband gets home from work

                I whisper *cardinal*
in his ear
and he puts on work gloves
takes the plastic bag from my hands

he has done this before
covered up the crimes committed

by our indoor-outdoor cat

he'll walk to the tree line and toss
the bird into the ocean of trees

he never complains about how
much this has taken out of him
out of us

when he comes back inside
I ask him about his day

it was a day he says   we're so tired, 16B0527
                                      trying to fix
                                      the unforgivable
                                      I'm sorry
                                      because I can't anymore
                                      and we fall asleep
he always says this

when I ask
and sometimes I ask
then say it before he does
and he shakes his head

later, when the cat wants to come in
it is my husband who opens the sliding glass door
asks him why he did what he did

gives him a little lecture
while he fills up his food bowl

when the cat finishes eating
he climbs up into my husband's lap
and lets him scratch behind his ears

my daughters have been painting
        what one-word messages
one-word messages on rocks:
        would you paint on rocks

Inspire
Hope
Love
Share
Trust
Forgiveness

my oldest is glad you are in prison
my youngest does not pronounce the r when she says *bird*

you have a botha my youngest asks
and my oldest looks at me and waits
for me to change the subject

I stopped letting my oldest write you letters
        maybe this is how
after her nightmares started
        we are burying you
I never told you
that she's afraid of you now
and you never ask
why she stopped writing

so much of what we say
is what we don't say

how a minute feels like a month to you
and for me a month goes by in a minute

my oldest was 7
now she's 11
my youngest was inside me
kicking
when you did what no one ever
believed
you could do
she'll be four
in a few months

she'll never know the you

I knew
just the monsterized you

the you
who I don't know how to grieve

a halo of red feathers mark
your grave, you are
dead
and alive
      you were taken
simultaneously
      and you took

you are presently absent
and absently present

I had a dream about you
you were hiding in the woods
behind my house
I left a bowl of cat food out

in the middle of the night
I watched you crawl
out of the woods to eat

I felt guilty for feeding you
as if you were a lie
that I should starve

then you crawled back
but by the time you made it
to the first line of trees
the woods turned into an ocean
and a wave crashed over you
and dragged you away
with seaweed tangled around your wrists

I often wish our father would appear
        you can drive yourself mad
in my dreams and explain why
        searching for an answer
this happened

before I go to bed
I pray to a god
I don't believe in
to bring him to me

he never appears

do you pray for answers
        or know them

I put a red feather under my pillow

he still does not come

when the cat scratches at the door

I pretend I don't hear him
like when the phone rings
and I see that it is you calling
and I decide to
go on doing
whatever it is
that I am doing

scratch

scratch

SCRatch

SCRATCHHHHHH

you have a collect call from an inmate
at a New York State Penitentiary
if you would like to accept charges
please
dial
one
now

you have to open yourself up
to forgive

I can't

I just
can't

what
you
DID

what
I
didn't

this isn't

it's

on a windy Thursday afternoon
my therapist suggests I finish the
letter I started

dear 16B0527
my therapist and I are working on
forgiveness
she says I should write you
but she doesn't tell me what
to say

your nieces hid the rock
that they painted the word "forgiveness" on
in some high grass
by the bank of the river
I wonder who will pick it up
hold the heaviness of forgiveness
in their hand before
tossing it
or taking it with them

I put the letter
in my desk drawer

I close my eyes
and visualize the words

      they come apart

      then back together

there is another inmate
with tattoos all over his face
he sits down in front of me

he asks me how I am
and I ask him who he is
it's me he says, *Steve*

stop lying to me
tell me what happened
to my little brother
tell me what happened
I need to go on

when our cat leaves mice
outside the door
I am silently grateful

how is one life
any less valuable
than another
why do I feel bad about everything I think now
as if our thoughts can be tried

I loved you I write
on a blank sheet of paper
crumbled it up
toss it
my words hit the rim of trashcan
then drop to the floor
they come apart

the
past
tense
of love
is
forgiveness

a robin on a Wednesday

Thursday a warbler
left by the door

would the guards allow you
the gift of
a feather
taped to
a blank sheet of paper
      would they allow you love

when I tell you I started
watching birds
you laughed

and said
you are watching birds
and I am doing bird

geese in autumn remind me of you
honking harbingers
signifying the end of one season
the beginning of another

and today long after the V of geese flew by
one straggler veered in the wrong direction

I watched him bob like a buoy in the sky

I thought about you

how you have to carry the weight of what you did

how I have to let that weight go

geese aren't known for leaving loved ones behind

maybe I was just too focused on the life
in front of me
and didn't see you veering off

maybe the others will come back for you
the ones who cut off contact
maybe they will show you the way

or maybe you will become a buoy
whose string was cut
by the blade of a boat or a malicious fisherman

maybe you will float further and further away
until you disappear

in a sea of
red feathers

or get caught up in your mind's net
a crueler prison
than the one you were sentenced to

I never thought I would allow myself
to go on without you

to fly further and further away
the cat is at the sliding glass door

we are looking at each other
the way we look at each other

you on the inside
and me on the outside

I let him in
he circles my leg

as he waits for me
to get his food
once it is in his bowl
he forgets all about me

do you ever miss me

or just your own life

I miss us

digging for clams
with our bare feet
in the Shinnecock Bay

warning one another
about
razor clams

don't step there
or there
or

then later
back at the house
that you shared with her
we shucked clams
and ate them raw

the way we did
when we were kids
we slurped them up
so fast
that dad couldn't open them
fast enough

you were always kind
and quiet
thoughtful
and helpful
not an animal
who could commit
such a heinous crime

you were my little brother

my best friend

the little boy who
wanted to be a fireman
the teen who wanted to be
an engineer
the adult who wanted to be
free of the voices
that no one else heard

prison changes people
my therapist says
as if I didn't know
imagine what he is going through

and I tell her
I thought about that
everyday
until I couldn't anymore
I tell her I came to her
to find forgiveness
she picks up her calendar
and tells me she will be
out of town
that next Thursday

yesterday, I forced my oldest daughter
to apologize to my youngest daughter
for an offense that I can't recall

say sorry I repeated
until she inaudibly mumbled the word
sorry

you said sorry to me
sort of
but it was as if the letters were
birds
startled by gunshots
flying in different directions

my oldest loves the blue jays
who travel together—

look the blue jays, she says,
when she spots them

I turn my head, but close my eyes

the blue jays remind me
of prison guards

the guards who walk you down corridors
in wrist and ankle chains
guards with guns
maybe lovers and children
brothers and sisters
mothers and fathers
maybe even wives
guards who have learned how
to identify other birds
who cannot fly
by their voices
who watch birds
stretching in the yard
birds sharpening shivs
birds being stalked by cats
guards who do nothing
when they should do something
and do something
when they should do nothing
guards
who watch
birds hiding contraband
birds fighting over worms
birds waiting for visitors
who never come

he has NO ONE
and I am annoyed
with how my subconscious
is trying to guilt me
into forgiveness
so I go swimming
and let the water

hold the weight of my worries
for a little while

but as I am doing laps
I can't help but think
of how you can't swim
for the next two decades
how we spent so much
of our childhood
in and around water

and I push myself harder
thinking about the ocean
of our childhood

remember how I saved you once

when you fell head first into a pool
and could not swim

I dreamt about that once
but it was the other way around

I was the one who fell
and forgot how to swim

and it was a stranger
who grabbed me and held
my head above water
it was stranger who said *just float*
remember what you taught me
let go, float

and then there was the time
not long after my fourth surgery
when we waded into the ocean
and a dead seagull
wrapped around your leg

it's an omen you said

you really said that

and I remember thinking what are the chances
of that happening to anyone

a seagull wrapping around your ankle like a chain

the entire Atlantic Ocean and it wrapped around

your leg

like a chain

an omen

if you believe in those sorts of things

could the tides be working against you
rising when you want them to fall

falling when you want them to rise

remember how dad always knew
the tides as if the chart was tattooed
on the back of his tar stained hands—

he worked so hard

always moving

always trying to make our lives better

this would kill your father our cousin said

after you did the unthinkable
and I said *thankfully you can't die twice*

but I was wrong

you, the you I thought I knew, died
that night in the house
by the lake

and the you, I don't want to know,
will die at an undisclosed time
in the future
possibly inside the deep dark depths
of the prison system
possibly dying as
16B0527
instead of my little brother

dear 16B0527
do you think after
we die we will come back

slip into the sea
become fish

fins or feather
blood or water

something that resembles
doing what is right
honorable
the way we were taught
to stand by one another

how dad loved bird watching
he kept a record in an identification book
complete with the date, time and
location of his sightings

a month after you graduated
from high school, he saw a

double-crested cormorant
in his favorite top-secret fishing spot

you are the only one who knows
all of his special spots
places he wouldn't tell anyone else about

will you draw me a map—
tell me where to bait my hook

I bought your youngest son
a magnetic fishing game
we sat on the couch
pretending it was a boat
                      do you reach for
and casted over the carpeted floor
                      your shadow

                            casted on the concrete walls
later on, we ate peanut butter and jelly sandwiches
that we pretended were the blue fish we caught

I want the world to make sense again

I want to able to look through old photo albums
without tears—

you holding a lobster

a bluefish

a striped bass

a snapper

a bushel of clams

an oyster you are shucking

a deer's antlers

a lunchbox

a bulldozer

a teddy bear

a pumpkin

a handful of leaves

a tree branch

a snowball

the hand of the woman you loved

my oldest daughter cradled in your arms
your oldest son cradled in your arms

your youngest son cradled in your arms

my waist as we ride on the back of an elephant

at the only circus we ever went to

all of these images captured forever—

reminders of times that made sense

in our mother's room, I saw a picture
of you and her in the visiting room
of the maximum-security prison
that you call home
I turned the photo around

I could not look into your eyes

they are the eyes of your sons

they are muddy puddles

that my daughters jump into

with their good shoes on

they are the edge
of the woods
in autumn

they are raw clams
on a half shell

they are the cat's eyes
watching a cardinal

they are cockroaches
scurrying in and out
of your cell

they are the tar
that stained dad's hands

I thought I would never turn away from you

I thought I would never

say I am an only child when asked

the cold weather is setting in fast

the way it does in upstate New York

yesterday was eighty degrees
today it won't reach sixty

tomorrow it could snow
in the higher elevations

we haven't closed the pool yet
it's 57 degrees out and I have to get in
to vacuum out the leaves
to pick up all the toys that sunk
to the bottom
before we winterize it

does it make you sad to know
I helped teach your sons
how to swim

that you won't be able to
jump into a body of water
for decades
that I saved you

I remember swimming
with you in the bay
in October
when we were kids

I remember
how warm the water was
compared to the cold air

we didn't know anything
about what was to come

we were just kids

growing up on an island

the only danger we knew
were hurricanes in autumn

boarding up windows

rising water

sitting in the dark

with candles
flashlights
a deck of cards

and then when the storm passed
driving around in dad's pickup
surveying the damage

a roofer loves high winds
shingles lifting from roofs
trees planted close to houses
leaks

like the one that let
forgiveness escape

like howling from the depths
of the prison system

your house is always noisy
and it drives you nuts
you would wear ear plugs
but that would be dangerous

I wish I knew how to
make forgiveness—
there is no book to open
no recipe to follow:

add one red feather
¼ cup love
a tablespoon of empathy

a teaspoon of love
a pinch of compassion

mix until there are no visible chunks,
then pour into a nine-inch pie dish
bake at 350 for one hour
let cool before serving

your birthday is coming
you will make
a jail house microwavable cake
with Oreo cookies,
M&Ms, Kool-Aid, and a Pepsi

you will share a slice with your bunkie
a man who has only eleven years
left of his sentence
a man who always beats you
in cards, a man who says he is
innocent, he didn't rape that woman
he wasn't even in town that weekend
he has proof, he is just waiting
on his appeal

you believe him

you don't ask me when
I am coming to visit
anymore

you have given up

it's been over a year
since I have seen you

the last time I saw you
I was still half-filled with forgiveness
we laughed about something

but I don't remember what
I just remember feeling guilty
that I could share laughter with you,
but her family can't share laughter with her

here's the thing
I can hear her laugh
it's one of those
that lingers
even during the worst days

sometimes her laugh is comforting

other times haunting

Halloween is coming—
I have pictures of you and her
on Halloween
you came to our old house
and we went trick-or-treating
with my oldest
who was a ladybug that year
she wore red rainboots, with
black polka-dots,
that were too big
for her feet

you took off your sock
and put it on foot
so that her boot
would stop slipping off

I have a picture of
my little ladybug
half of your body is in the frame

I cut
you

out

I don't want anyone to ask
who is that
it's easier to make you disappear
completely

I just want to put on gloves
walk what you did
to the edge of the woods
and toss it as far as I can

I have pictures of us
from Halloweens past
snapshots of our childhood

a lion and a mouse
a ghost and a princess

a robot and a clown

an astronaut and an alien

a ninja and a punk rocker

a cowboy and a punk rocker

a werewolf and a punk rocker
this year my daughters were going as
a witch and a black cat

but then they decided
on super girl and an attendee at a masquerade ball
what you gonna be mommy
my little one asks

and I say *happy*

because what else is there to be

today it is raining

again

if only the rain
were forgiveness

I would tip my head
open my mouth
and collect forgiveness
fill that empty space
inside me

she's been sick for three days
straight, things are growing
inside of her that shouldn't be—

I read somewhere that
anger can do this—
make you literally sick

I could die in here, you said
right after the plea bargain
and sentencing when they moved you
from county jail to
a maximum-security prison

all the men growing like disease
inside the walls of the prison,
they don't belong there

but maybe they do
no one wants to talk about certain systems—

prisons

SENTENCING MEMORANDUM

ppearing before Your Honor for sentencing after

or

reproductive

either you are producing or you are silenced

I haven't talked to you about the cancer
growing on her uterine wall
how your old room
is filling up with inmates

about the scheduled hysterectomy

about how she is all that I have left

how scared she is
how could you do this

one night
drunken
and delusional
in a house
by a lake
in a house
where everyone
was happy the day before

a house where
your son took his mommy's lipstick
and drew all over the floors
the day before
you lost your mind

you laughed about it
and told her the floor
needed the lipstick more
than she did
she was beautiful the way she

was

I had a dream
I was rowing a boat
on a lake of red feathers
and heard a woman screaming
then the boat sprung
a leak

I had another dream
where you were flying
in air, but you weren't
you were swimming
well not really swimming
you were drowning
but it wasn't even you
it was a black cat
adrift in an ocean

how did we get here

talk to me
tell me what happened
why you did what you did

stop telling me you can't remember
stop telling me you thought someone
was going to kill you, that they were talking
in Russian, that they followed you home,
waited until you were asleep then came for you

you were always afraid someone
or something
was coming for you

and the saddest part
is we normalized your paranoia
because the human conscience

is bordered by woods

no one thought much of
your plans to build a bunker
in the woods behind mom's house
and stockpile supplies
for emergency purposes

I laughed when you told me to get a gun
I'll shoot my eye out, I said
but you didn't laugh
you were serious
you told me I had to protect myself

from who I asked

maybe forgiveness is a feather
a red one
one left by the backdoor
one my youngest picks up
and says *so pity mom, so pity*
and she is right

it is a pity

that red feather resting
in her little hand
like a crooked smile

the *r* she can't pronounce

drop it I tell her
there can be lice on that
you can't bring that inside

she drops the feather
and her smile tumbles
to the ground

I am trying to keep
the invaders out

I am afraid of everything
now

I am trying not to be afraid

I don't want my daughters to be afraid

I can't sleep mommy, I just can't fall asleep

I am always looking
for the other feather
to drop
this year's first frost warning
came after a week with three days
above eighty degrees

the wolf spiders
are uninvited house guests
coming in droves
through cracks under doorways

like the voices
that invade your mind
you can't put a towel
under the entrance
of your ears and block
the voices
you can't cover your eyes
and make whatever
you see go away
it's already inside

and you don't know how
and when it entered
and you don't know how

to get it to leave

because it isn't
a shapeshifter

your son drew an arrow
on the floor
with his mother's lipstick

the arrow pointed
toward the lake

you got on your hands and knees
and screamed why
when you realized what
you did
you tried to go back to sleep
go back into the dream
so you would wake up
somewhere else

they hide in the folds of your thoughts
and multiply
in the cobwebbed corners of your imagination

eight legs stretched around your skull

tell me that you were just angry
that would be easier to understand

and I need to make sense of this
senselessness

I need to know that I knew you
before I didn't

I bring my girls to a fall festival
at an orchard

they zigzag around trees
looking for the largest apples

they are beautiful

they hold hands

pull each other in different directions

there is a petting zoo
insatiable goats
ducklings
sheep
one bunny

there is a hay maze
and my daughters
run through it a dozen times
with their friend
who finds a woolly bear caterpillar
and hands it to her mother
who rolls it around her hand
and says *it's not doing too good,
I'll throw it over the fence
for the birds*
and my daughter's friend shrieks
it's the circle of life, her mother says
and other mothers look on in disgust
as the leaves on the trees around them
are writing their own elegies

these mothers nervously change
the subject, remark about how
gorgeous the foliage is

my brother killed the woman he said he loved

there's a band playing

and a muddy hill
where my youngest joins
other kids who are rolling
      rolling
           rolling
like the
flaming maple leaves
blowing in the wind
being fanned by the yellow ginko
red oak, sassafras,
spreading like wild fire
tupelo
sugar maple
tamarack
bigtooth aspen
bitternut hickory
witch hazel
and river birch

red leaf feathers

and cancer

god, it is so beautiful here in the fall

my daughters are laughing

and the sun is here

I talked to you a few hours before you killed her
you were drunk
and I told you not to drive

in the spring,
the surviving woolly caterpillars will thaw
feed again, pupate, create a cocoon
and emerge as the Isabella Tiger moth

in contrast
it is Sunday
and you will spend 23 and a half hours
surrounded by concrete and steel
a dismal landscape that will
never welcome change
and thirty minutes outside in the yard
you will do this each day for
the next twenty-something years

and if you survive
you will emerge into a world
that kept changing
while you remained frozen

and you will still be my brother
but you won't be the brother I know
or knew or thought I knew
you'll be radically different
in ways I won't understand

I canceled therapy this week
I am losing faith
forgiveness will have to wait
until my next appointment

everything is growing
her cancer
my fears
my children
your children
                                       the name of days
the distances between us
                                       have become numbers

                                       just like the inmates
it's Friday

if you open a wall
be prepared to gut your house

I have learned that
and relearned that
several times

I am getting quite good at
making the seams disappear

if I forgive you,
if I go
stop
looking for answers

It's Saturday morning
my oldest and I are up
watching cartoons and eating
crispy Chinese noodles
that we dip in duck sauce

this is our first meal of the day
and we take our time
one crispy noodle at a time

I love her in a way I never
loved myself—

that's what children do
they make you love more
than you thought you ever could
this joy will never be yours—

your sons will never know you

they will create their own versions of you
in your absence

they wear your mannerisms like
a bird wears it feathers
they make me want to scream
no
No
nO
fly higher!

it's difficult to watch you
in your sons

the rough bark of your eyes
looking into me

just as I realize the noodles
aren't sitting well in my belly
my daughter says
I don't think that was a good idea
and curls up next to me
like a regret
and I wonder what it would be like
not having her here
with me
but knowing she was alive
somewhere else
growing up without me

wearing my eyes
thin hair and stubby nose
and I curl up next to her
like a pardon

a leaf dangling on a branch
on a windy day

and think about what it would be like
       they were just three and one
if she died and I had to go on

without her

a leaf falling from a branch
tumbling in the wind

and she pushes into me
        they were just babies
like I can make the pain go away
        eggs abandoned in a nest
and I push into her like she can
        make my pain go away

and then I say, *I feel like I have to fart
so bad, but I can't*

me too, she says

and we laugh so hard

that she farts

then we laugh harder

the smell of healing
isn't always pleasant

                                          I feel guilty
when I laugh—

                and I didn't do anything

                      wrong

it is Thursday
and I am sitting in her office
and she is asking me questions

that don't even reference you
and I want to talk about you
but I don't want to bring you up

my therapist talks about herself
and I wonder if I should start
charging her for my time
I wonder if this is worth it
talking about all the things
that I can't change

it's 2am
now it's 1am
daylight savings
and your birthday was three days ago
the card I finally wrote you
is still here
on my desk
and when you call I tell you
about the card unsent

thank you
you say

and you tell me how
you were moved to honor block
how you had your first eggbeater and bacon sandwich on a bagel
in years
how they leave the cell doors open
you can walk around and talk to the other men
play cards
you got a 98 on a test for a class you are taking
you feel a little bit
kind of
sort of
humanish

part of me is happy for you

and the other part
is angry
you took
so much
from so many

when you were free
we would call one another
on every birthday
and sing off-key

I don't dare sing to you now

mom said she went to visit
you played cards
and ate a chicken sandwich
from the vending machine
she said you look good
but you drifted off a lot
she had to call your name
tell you it was your turn

not too many people send you letters
anymore, besides a few family friends
our high school biology teacher
the best teacher we had
a man who fell off a roof
while he was cleaning a chimney
a man now a prisoner in his own body

it is funny how sometimes what happens
helps us understand others a little better

I tell you how I rode the Herschell-Spillman Carousel
on the fourth floor at the state museum
with your sons this past weekend,
how the forty animals that predate the machinery and

platform consist of 36 horses in varying sizes and poses
two donkey and two deer
then before you can speak
I tell you how
our neighbor shot
a rabid raccoon
in our front yard
the other day
how the gunshot
startled my husband
who was outside working

and before you can respond
our time is up, someone else
is waiting for the phone
and you have to return to
your long unpunctuated sentence

your youngest son giggled
the entire time
we rounded the terrace
but your oldest didn't smile once
he just looked off
into his own spinning world

I kneel down on the floor
the phone still in hand
the dead line beeping

remember the lobsters
how happy we were
when the pots
dad set out
were full

all those shellfish
trying to claw their way out

rubber bands
used as shackles
to prevent a fight

we'd wait for the water to boil
toss them into
the giant steaming pot
on the stove top

there is a noise
of air expanding
that sounds like a scream

but they have no throats
no vocal chords
 and remember how they thrash about
for the first few minutes

how when they turn the perfect
shade of red, you pick them up

plate them
crack their hard shells
to get to their soft meat

I forgive you
I forgive you
I
can't help thinking about you
thrashing around in your cell
like a lobster in boiling water
knowing that even if you
get out
after all those years
you won't be able survive

not for long

you'll be a lobster out of water

but you might argue
that a lobster carries
its home with him
the way we carry
the exoskeleton of our past

you can lose everything
accept your mind

I am cleaning every crevice
of my mind with a cracker
and pick, I am dropping it
in butter. I am waiting for my bowl
to be full
I want you to know
that I wish I could do better than this

I am wearing one of your sweatshirts
right now, I am thinking about how
we dragged your life out into the road
and left a free sign there
within an hour everything was gone

If you could do this
anyone is capable of anything
this thought terrifies me

because you can't see
the things you should fear most

this afternoon, I asked my oldest
to mend a pair of boots for my youngest,
she pulled out her sewing box
and within an hour, she had redesigned
the boots

with pompoms and buttons
and I tell you this not because you can relate
but because you can't and
this makes me sad

to survive
I have to let you go

forgiveness
is that weird contraption
that she uses to
thread her needle
and I watched her
so focused on each stitch
and this is enough
this is all I need
what are you doing right now
I mean right this second
what are you doing

are you pretending to sleep
or asleep and if you are
what do you dream about
are you always free in your dreams

I am coming to see you in a few weeks
I won't tell you
I will just show up

I will search for any excuse
to change my mind

I will talk this over with my therapist
tomorrow
she will tell me to
visualize visiting you
to prepare myself
she will tell me about her life

and I will wonder why
I keep going to see her

I wish we could carry our homes
with us like lobsters
molt when we outgrow them
no sheetrock, no screws and nails
no painting
no barbwire, no locks and steel bars
no cell tossing

do you remember the wall paper
in the living room of our house
on sixth street or that
wood burning stove
I touched more than once
even after the first burn

do you remember how dad once
put down a few lobster on the floor
of that room and let us play
with them for a little while
before dinner
like they were puppies

maybe we do or can
carry our homes with us
maybe our homes are
the color of lobsters before
being boiled, the color of a
heart beating in the chests
of all the men
who live under the same
roof as you

how different are any of us
from one another anyhow

if we are looking from the inside out
instead of the outside in

and then I am in her office
and she draws a diamond
and asks me to write
all the good and bad aspects
of you on the sides of this three-dimensional shape
and I say I don't like this metaphor
and then she says write
how you are feeling around the
diamond and I write

pissed off
tricked
alone
tired
embarrassed

and then she asks
if I have grieved for you

and I say *yes*
I have cried

and she tells me that crying is not grieving
then she tells me about her neighbor
and how she put one of those
little free libraries in her front yard

outside there is a birdhouse
in a balding tree

it reminds me of your receding hair line
an ocean pushing further and further
away from the shore

and I also write

sometimes I wish you would disappear

what do you mean disappear she asks

and I say I mean that if you died
I would feel relieved

the vacant birdhouse sways in the wind
the womb we both inhabited
now empty and afraid
the cracking of lobster shells to get to the meat
the way I tell her that I am going to visit you
in two weeks

I have to figure out how to forgive
you
                    for the unthinkable
and myself
                         for all that I can't change

I was always the bad example

I wrote you a letter three weeks ago
for your birthday and I still
haven't written your address on the envelope

I included a picture of your sons
with my daughters in Halloween costumes

  it's not fair   two
  beautiful   orphan boys

       a vampire   and
bat man   two boys
     who will never know   the you I loved
how you sobbed after your first son was born
  because you could rock a part of you to sleep now

two capes
plastic fangs
a super hero mask

when I come visit
you will ask me about the sons you'll never get to see

if I decided not to visit you ever again
I will still see you every time I look
into your sons' eyes

the grieving process is nonlinear

outside I hear the honking of geese
the cold is closing in on us

and I am not ready for the long winter
                      to be locked in

do you ever think about how we ice skated on that pond
when we lived on Manor Lane
the burn barrel
all those boys playing hockey and me
      how they were all surprised when they got
checked by a chick
                                   how the ice
creaked sometimes   or puddles
would form on the top
      how the older kids would hide cheap beer in the woods
how you started using my stick
when I started going to parties
in lieu of playing hockey

last winter, I brought your sons ice skating for the first-time
      I held their hands to steady them
            and when I thought they were ready
                  I let go

                   and they fell
                          again and again

we were walking across that thing we shared
water

and I could hear that cracking noise
but I wasn't afraid
              this was a manmade rink, less than a
foot deep
ice

I don't remember learning to skate
I just remember how I was the only one
who played hockey in figure skates

that thin blade   choice
all the minutes   in each day
and how we spend them

the way my laced fingers look like a nest
and forgiveness an egg
that small boy in the tree stand waiting

did I tell you
                                     are they listening
did I

it gets dark
early
here
now?

Rebecca Schumejda is the author of several full-length collections including *Falling Forward* (sunnyoutside press), *Cadillac Men* (NYQ Books), *Waiting at the Dead End Diner* (Bottom Dog Press) and most recently *Our One-Way Street* (NYQ Books). She is the co-editor at Trailer Park Quarterly. She received her MA in Poetics from San Francisco State University and her BA from SUNY New Paltz. She lives in New York's Hudson Valley with her family. You can find her online at: rebecca-schumejda.com

Hosho McCreesh is currently writing, painting, and making stuff in the gypsum & caliche badlands of the American Southwest. His work has appeared widely in print, audio, & online. He can be found at www.hoshomccreesh.com

www.ingramcontent.com/pod-product-compliance
Lightning Source LLC
Chambersburg PA
CBHW041313110526
44591CB00022B/2897